# Baby Tips
*for new moms*

First
4 Months

# Baby Tips™
## *for new moms*

# First
# 4 Months

JEANNE MURPHY

FISHER
BOOKS.

Publishers:       Bill Fisher
                  Helen V. Fisher
                  Howard W. Fisher

Managing Editor: Sarah Trotta

Cover Design:     FifthStreet*design*, Berkeley, CA

Production:       Deanie Wood
                  Randy Schultz
                  Josh Young

Cover Illustration: © 1998 Sharon Howard Constant

Illustrations:    Cathie Lowmiller

Published by
Fisher Books, LLC
5225 W. Massingale Road
Tucson, Arizona 85743-8416
(520) 744-6110

Trade edition     ISBN 1-55561-166-4
Printing 5

Special edition   ISBN 1-55561-211-3
Printing 5 4 3 2 1

Printed in the U.S.A.

**Library of Congress Cataloging-in-Publication Data**
Murphy, Jeanne, 1964-
    [Baby tips for new moms, first 4 months]
    Jeanne Murphy's baby tips for new moms,
      first 4 months.
        p.   cm.
    Includes index.
    ISBN 1-55561-166-4
    1. Infants. 2. Infants—Care. 3. Infants—
      Development. 4. Mother and infant.   I. Title
    HQ774.M89  1998
    649'. 122—dc21                          98-6319
                                            CIP

To pass along your own helpful suggestions to
new mothers for future editions of this book,
please call (800) 617-4603.

*Notice:* The information in this book is true and complete to the best of our knowledge. It is offered with no guarantees on the part of the author or Fisher Books. Author and publisher disclaim all liability in connection with the use of this book.

The suggestions made in this book are opinions and are not meant to supersede a doctor's recommendation in any way. Always consult your doctor before beginning any new program.

# Contents

# Introduction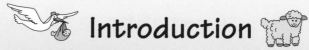

**Congratulations**—you have a new baby! Don't worry too much about caring for the newest member of your family. Infants mainly need your love, assistance and genuine interest in learning their needs. I have collected all the enclosed tips and tricks from my own experiences and from my own mother. I sincerely hope that some of them will help you through these first few months of learning. God bless you and enjoy every moment—it really does go by too fast!

*Jeane*

# First Month

Happy Birthday, baby, and welcome to the world!

Sweet baby, this world may not seem as warm as the place you became used to for nine months. But it **can** be, and with the help of this book, we hope it **will** be.

Rule #1: Don't believe everything you hear or read. Not even this book! What do I know? Take what proves useful and leave the rest behind.

# Well-baby checkups are done at:

| | |
|---|---|
| 2 weeks | 9 months |
| 1 month | 12 months |
| 2 months | 15 months |
| 4 months | 18 months |
| 6 months | 24 months |

—and at each birthday that follows, until your doctor says you are excused.

Warm those cold diaper wipes in your hand before you change your baby!

Also, use a diaper wipe. The people who say you can save money by **not** using a wipe at diaper changes are forgetting the additional cost of the doctor visit when the baby gets a rash or fungus.

This is an old wives' tale, but . . . burp your baby after every 3 ounces of liquid. If the baby doesn't burp by the time you count to 300, lay him flat on his back for 60 seconds. Then pick him up and resume burping him while you are standing. (He'll burp then!)

Keep a bib on your baby even when she isn't eating. (Babies spit up at the most unexpected times.)

Leave tags on all the baby gifts you receive until you use them. Babies grow fast. If you can't use some items (or you have duplicates), you can return them unused for something else you do need. Or the items may make perfect gifts for someone else. (This helps if you are busy and can't get out to shop later.)

If you notice you are missing a button or you've dropped something equally small, make a point to check baby's mouth and hands right away.

Adjust your water heater to a maximum of 120F or 49C. That way, you can't accidentally scald your baby with the bath or tap water.

Don't put a monitor next to baby's head or too close to your head. Put it elsewhere in the room. Don't keep the volume too high, because if you do, baby's frequent stirs and yawns are sure to keep you awake.

$C$onsider the expression "adjustment period" as the time baby needs to get accustomed to your family's schedule, **not** the time your family needs to adjust to his schedule.

The more your baby feels loved, the happier she usually is. Hug your new baby and tell her you love her as often as you can, especially if she is crying. Remember, your baby is trying to reach out to you and communicate without knowing how to talk.

Air your baby daily. The best way to handle diaper rash is for your baby not to get it. Five minutes a day without a diaper really helps!

Babies like to be bounced gently, not shaken or patted too hard. Shaking or patting a baby too hard can severely injure him—or worse.

Let your baby eat until he stops. As a rule, try to feed your newborn baby at least 3 ounces at a time. If he does  not drink enough, he will be hungry continuously. And if he does drink enough, he will sleep better at night.

I think babies can see in the dark because they're used to it.

Try not to make abrupt moves around your infant. Startled babies create a crying frenzy.

Place a slow-moving fan in baby's room to circulate air. Turn it on each time you put your baby down to sleep. She will become conditioned to sleeping when she hears this noise—handy when you're on vacation or visiting someone else's home. Babies can learn to sleep deeply with background noises. Be sure not to point the fan at the baby.

Every now and then **don't** turn on the fan, so your baby will also be able to sleep when a fan isn't available.

$B$abies cry when they are hungry, wet, bored, sick, tired or just to relieve stress . . . so do postpartum moms!

Try to get your baby used to sleeping **anywhere** from an early age. Don't always use the crib or bassinet for his naps. For example, from Day One, let him take every other afternoon nap in the playpen in a busy room (such as the family room) with the TV on.

Placing a blanket around your baby in the crib will make him feel more secure and comfortable. Roll up the blanket and encircle your baby closely with it, especially when he is a newborn.

If you happen to end up with two or three baby monitors, don't return them immediately. Think: living room, master bedroom, kitchen, grandmother's house. Use them all! (This way you avoid having to move them around the house.)

Is your baby a light sleeper? You will need to teach her that just because she wakes up rarin' to go whenever someone goes by, it doesn't mean that person intends to pick her up and take her out for a walk.

Keep burned-out light bulbs in their sockets until they are replaced, so baby won't be tempted to put a finger in the electrical socket. Keep lamps out of baby's reach to prevent accidental burns.

Become aware of these hazards now, before your baby is active enough to discover them himself.

Don't wake your baby to change a diaper unless she has had a bowel movement and really needs it. (Good diapers are designed to handle these situations and last for hours.)

$G$etting a baby to sleep through the night is like testing the deep end of a pool. Prepare yourself mentally and venture a little further each night. Good news—eventually, you will make it!

Try this: Each night, from now until the baby catches on, plan to put him to bed for the night at 11 p.m.—not 7 p.m. Give him a bath at 10:30 p.m., play together a little and then, after he's been stimulated and fed, put him down to sleep for good. Your goal should be to train baby to sleep the 12 a.m.–5 a.m. shift **first**.

If your infant cries every time you put him down, try warming a blanket in the dryer first and then put him down on it. He will probably love it and quiet immediately.

Remember this trick when you are moving your baby from the bassinet into his crib, and if you want your baby to take a nap when you are visiting friends.

$S$trive to put your newborn baby into the crib instead of the bassinet at night by six weeks of age. (You don't want her to become too used to the bassinet.) By eight weeks, your baby will be ahead of the game for sleeping through the night—and she will love having her own place.

Let your newborn baby sleep! It depends on the baby of course, but more likely than not, your baby can sleep all day at this age and then sleep just as well at night. Check on her regularly, and I say, if she's OK, you're OK!

If your baby falls asleep in the car, take him out of the car seat as soon as you get home and put him into his own bed. This simple practice will remind baby that he **can** go back to sleep after being moved. After all, he did it in the womb!

Do not use a pillow, puffy comforter or lamb's-wool mattress cover in your baby's crib until she is old enough to lift her head and hold it up. Studies prove that these items contribute to sudden infant death syndrome, or SIDS. Also, try putting your baby down to sleep on her back. If your baby objects, discuss it with your doctor.

$D$on't worry, Mom—it takes 9 months to put on the pounds, so give yourself at least 9 months to take them off. Drink lots of water and you'll be fine.

Bathing an infant before bed calms him. Feed him a warm bottle or nurse him after each bath and he may actually sleep longer.

# Second Month

$B$e efficient. Sterilize enough nipples and prepare and pour formula into enough bottles to last 48 hours instead of 24. Presto—You've eliminated half of this work!

If your baby just looks at you without expression, even when you are trying to get him to smile, he is probably concentrating. He may be studying something new about your face. Or he may be having a bowel movement.

He is **not** thinking you are an idiot.

Before calling your doctor's office with a concern about your baby, be sure you know baby's temperature. Your doctor will usually ask about this right away. Doctors usually prefer a rectal reading.

If your baby rubs her eyes **or** moves her head back and forth, she's probably trying to say, "No, not this activity. Let's try something else and I'll be fine. If I'm not, give me a nap please."

From the very beginning, babies learn to cry in different tones when they want different things. Watch for these distinguishing cries and you will learn what they need. (Most important, you will also be able to tell the difference between their normal needs and when they are in pain.)

If you don't want anyone to touch your baby, that's OK. If you can't seem to say so directly, just say the baby isn't feeling well and you don't want to risk spreading a virus.

Let your baby finish his bowel movement before you change his diaper. Unless he has diarrhea, by giving him a few minutes you will save yourself a lot more diaper-changing.

Don't turn on lights during night feedings. It may wake your baby.

A night-light in the room may keep your baby from sleeping deeply. Try using a nearby bathroom or hallway light instead while you are checking on your baby, and keep his room dark.

When your child passes gas, he burps out the other end.

Baby Tips

Babies wiggle! And for that reason, a baby will fall off of any counter he is put on. Always place babies safely on the floor, no matter what kind of carrying device or seat they are secured in.

Mom, are you stressed out? Consider this: Standard airline procedure tells parents to place an emergency oxygen mask over our own mouths first, if extra oxygen is needed in the cabin. Only after that are we to put a mask over our child's mouth. Only after **our** needs are met are we

**physically able** to take care of our child's needs.

It's not too different at home. For the family to be happy, Mom needs to take care of herself as well as her family. . . . Get some fresh air now and then!

From the very first day, children keep their own schedules. They do some things the same way, every day—like bowel movements, for example. Watch for the schedule and you will learn to relax. And if you help keep your child on her schedule, she will be more content.

The Golden Rule of sleeping through the night is this: If you turn on the TV or entertain your baby late at night **even once,** your baby will expect you to entertain him **every night** at that same time.

$\mathsf{K}$eep in mind that babies are actually around nine months old the day they are born!

Keep the components of a formula bottle together in one place. Use all the components every time you prepare a bottle. The cap prevents infection and is just as important as the nipple.

If you are an uptight parent, you probably have an uptight baby. If this is true for you, take 10 deep breaths and remember to smile at your baby every time you look at him.

Accidentally schedule your six-week doctor's appointment during a Monday-night football game and plan to go alone. (Oops!)

A child doesn't really "hate" anything. Things like the crib or the bouncing seat may just frighten him at first because he is unsure of it. Teach your baby to enjoy these things by introducing them at a slow, comfortable pace.

Baby Tips

If you throw a party or some other event, remember the baby is not used to so much company. She may become overstimulated from all the different people who want to hold her. At some point, go into a quiet room, remove her diaper, clothes and socks and give her some quiet space for 20 minutes. This works great and will revitalize her for another round!

Every home with a baby should have two infant bulb syringes . . . one for noses and one for ears. They are made differently and have different uses.

The nose syringe is especially helpful because you can clear a baby's nose with it just before feeding. He'll drink better, especially when he is sick.

Try putting your baby into a bouncing seat or car seat at an early age. Place the seat inside her playpen for a few minutes now and then. She will get used to the playpen this way. By the time she is ready for it, your baby will love spending lots of time playing in her "special" place.

If your baby gets diaper rash frequently, try changing diaper brands. Also, let your baby go diaperless regularly. The longer, the better (at least 10 minutes every waking hour is a tremendous help).

Prevention has its benefits! Remember, airing out your baby's bottom for just 5 minutes a **day** helps avoid diaper rash. Once your baby has a diaper rash, you'll need to air out his bottom at least 10 minutes **per hour** to get rid of it.

$P$ut down the baby! If you hold your baby too much, he'll never learn how to crawl or be alone.

$O$bserve your child for signs of individuality. For example, one of my boys liked to be completely undressed and was miserable unless his feet were free. The other one had to be completely bundled up at all times.

If your newborn isn't used to the swing yet, don't give up! Try again—and again! Babies change every day.

Babies usually love the sound of running water, so bring your baby into the bathroom in a carrying seat while you take a shower. He will probably fall asleep. Later, all that running water helps with potty training.

Turn on the water and you are on your way to training!

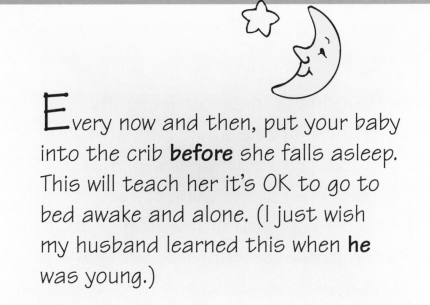

Every now and then, put your baby into the crib **before** she falls asleep. This will teach her it's OK to go to bed awake and alone. (I just wish my husband learned this when **he** was young.)

You **can** fool mother nature once in a while! Sucking is instinctive. So if your baby drank a bottle at 10 p.m. and was put to bed, try feeding her again at 11:30 p.m., even if she is sleeping. If she eats now, **you** may catch some uninterrupted sleep until 5 a.m. and avoid a middle-of-the-night feeding.

Don't overdress your baby just to visit a friend or go to the grocery store. How would **you** like it if you had to wear a business suit on your day off? Keep your baby comfortable and your life will be the same.

$S$leep when your baby sleeps.

Although sometimes it seems to take an eternity for a newborn to finish drinking his bottle, believe me, the slower, the better! Infants who drink too fast suffer from unbearable gas.

Remember: "gulp = gas."

Generally speaking, it takes 20 minutes or so to nurse or bottle-feed your newborn baby, excluding burping.

# Third Month

I don't think the sizes in children's clothing mean **anything**. For example, my son weighed 14 pounds at three months, but my nephew weighed 9 pounds. Which 3-month-old did the tag refer to? Don't miss the joy of seeing your baby in a cute outfit because he outgrew it too fast. Try on everything early and disregard the tags.

Your baby has guardian angels and smiles at them all the time. Have you noticed?

$B$abies cry just as hard when they are tired and want to go to bed as they do when they are hungry and want to eat.

After a baby has been crying uncontrollably for a little while, she may have forgotten **why** she is crying. Try rocking, dancing or singing. And stay calm!

Sometimes a music box can actually distress a baby or wake her up, especially after a long day. Instead, sing your baby a soft lullaby. Save the music box for times when baby plays in the crib during the day.

If you put your baby down for a nap at someone else's house, try to put the portable crib in the same position it would be at your house (such as facing the bedroom door, window on the left, and so on). Put your baby's head in the same place it would be in the crib at home. Then, turn on the fan!

If baby's nose is stuffy, he will be unable to drink or sleep soundly. Check with his doctor. Use a humidifier in his room, and hold him up in a sitting position while he is trying to drink.

In the third month, baby is getting ready for an activity. Best type of toy: One that hangs just high enough above her that she can learn how to kick and swat at things.

Instead of trying to keep the house silent while the baby sleeps, keep house noises at a normal level. Your baby will learn how to sleep through anything!

Don't try to reinvent the wheel. If you have friends who are mothers, take their advice. It saves a lot of time and upset.

If your baby is not sleeping well at night, instead of dressing her warmly, make the room a little warmer, and then dress her very lightly (in a "onesie" perhaps).

$G$et a mobile if you don't have one! Babies love to watch them and they're great for developing hand-foot coordination. The best mobile I've seen features frames made out of little cookie-cutter shapes. The frames can hold a picture of each member of your family.

Baby Tips

Be sure to remove the mobile the minute your baby learns to stand up, because mobiles are dangerous when a baby can reach them from the crib.

$S$terilize bottle nipples in boiling water for five minutes after each use for baby's first four months.

Baby Tips

$S$ome family members, especially grandparents, genuinely want to become close to your baby. Don't deprive your child or your relatives of this joy. Besides all its other benefits, the relationship will help your child learn how to love others.

$C$heck baby at bedtime. Roll back his sleeves if they might cover his hands in the night. This way, he won't wake up later because he cannot get to his thumb or hand to soothe himself.

Infants know who they are when they look into the mirror.

Is your baby suddenly very hungry all the time? If you are considering feeding your baby oatmeal or rice this early, keep in mind that growth spurts don't last very long. Give this stage a week or two and call your doctor before you make any decisions.

The same is true for the reverse of the growth spurt, when baby seems to eat less than usual for a while. And of course, sometimes baby is just not hungry. (I wish I were like that!)

If you plan to have professional photographs taken of your child:

1. Don't go to the studio on a holiday, weekend or during the lunch hour.

2. Arrange to go at 10:30 a.m., 2:30 p.m. or after 7:30 p.m.

3. One hour ahead of time: Feed your baby enough so she won't spit up or be irritable during the photo session.

4. Dress up your baby only when the child ahead of you is almost done.

If you plan a night out with your husband, don't use it as an opportunity to call a family grievance meeting. Save it for the next morning and enjoy yourself!

Relax—By the time your child is about to drive you crazy with some new and unique behavior, he will change his pattern to something else.

If your husband is acting more like a baby than your baby, baby him!

Baby Tips

Feed baby half of what she normally drinks. Then stop, change and burp her (even if it means waking her up). After that, finish the feeding. This way, she won't fall asleep before she is finished eating and she will be more likely to enjoy a longer rest.

As store-bought nipples become sticky, replace them. Worn-out nipples keep the baby from drinking smoothly, which will frustrate her.

It's also a good idea to leave newer nipples with your baby-sitter. It avoids the frustration problem, which the sitter may not recognize as such.

Leaving a baby in a car (running or not, locked or unlocked), is considered abuse and may be reported to the Division of Youth and Family Services (DYFS).

Always leave your doctor's number and the local poison-control center number with your baby-sitter. Also, leave a signed form that gives the person you deem responsible adequate medical authorization for your child's treatment in your absence.

Babies get bored quickly, but there **is** an upside: For example, you can use the swing for 15 minutes and then use it again 15 minutes later. It still works!

If your child is sick and does not sleep, he may be over-medicated. (Watch decongestants—some contain antihistamines or are high in sugar, which keeps the baby awake.)

Also, observe your child for any other reaction to medicine.

If you leave your child for more than 24 hours with a baby-sitter, don't be surprised if he treats the baby-sitter like his mother and you like his baby-sitter for 24 hours after you return. It's normal; babies adjust to their environment. Instead of feeling unhappy, be glad your baby is so adaptable!

Thoughts on baby monitors:

1. If your monitor is battery-powered, you don't have to plug it in.

2. Make sure you are listening to **your** child. Sometimes your baby monitor may pick up other people's monitors. (To test the monitor when you are alone, turn on a music box.)

3. Also remember that other people's monitors may pick up **yours.** Your best bet is to behave with your child as if someone else is listening.

$G$ive your home an early safety check. See it from your baby's viewpoint! For instance, check out your fireplace. Keep those heavy fire pokers and other dangerous accessories out of baby's reach. Remove matches or other fire starters. If you have a gas fireplace, remove the gas key.

You'll be glad you did later.

$C$onsider your baby a video camcorder with a high-tech recording system. **Everything you say is being registered.** Your words, thoughts and expressions will be replayed for you at a later date.

The best way to wake up your baby so he won't be grouchy is to turn off the fan or gently open the blinds about 15 minutes before you want to get going. (By the way, closing the blinds while baby is sleeping may help him sleep better too.)

Keep cords from blinds and curtains out of baby's reach, because they are choking and strangulation hazards.

If you know you will be converting entirely from nursing to bottle-feeding on a certain date, introduce the bottle only a few days in advance. Babies catch on remarkably fast. This way, the only "nipple confusion" you experience will be which one to buy.

All babies are good; some just cry more than others.

Baby Tips

# Fourth Month

If you see your child "chewing" instead of sucking, immediately wipe out her mouth with your finger to see if she has anything in there she shouldn't.

If your baby can hold up his head and support his weight while sitting, get the highchair ready: He is probably ready for solid foods!

Keep hot beverages out of baby's arm's-length reach. You don't realize how quick babies are until they have spilled something hot and burned themselves.

Whenever I think of cat naps, I think of my grandfather—on a hammock on the front porch or in a glider swing. Wherever I found him, he was always napping peacefully!

If your baby likes cat naps too—dozing off here and there instead of sleeping deeply—give him lots of fresh air. Try using a portable swing (they even come in a glider style).

Leave the baby-sitter exact instructions for reaching you in an emergency. Don't call the baby-sitter every hour after you go out. If you don't think your sitter is capable enough to use the instructions, don't leave your child with that sitter.

In 1999, the reasonable rate for a baby-sitter is $3.50 per hour for one child, $5.00 per hour for two.

Try filing baby's nails instead of cutting them, especially if your personal style is more like a bull in a china shop than a ballerina.

It is easier to file or cut nails when babies are sleeping.

When using a dropper for baby medicine, place the end of the dropper **under** the baby's tongue and dispense the medicine. If you try to dispense the medicine on top of her tongue, she will spit it out.

Babies get cranky from overstimulation. So do adults!

Warm bottles are wonderful. They go down easy, and they put babies right to sleep. But do give a room-temperature or even a cold bottle to your baby every now and then. Baby will find it strange. But it will prevent a major problem if you are caught unprepared later, when you can't make the bottle "just right" for some reason.

As he grows, your baby will be able to eat more. You will notice he will find it easier to sleep longer now. You can put him down to sleep earlier and earlier. Eventually you will be able to enjoy 10 to 12 uninterrupted hours if you do it consistently! This should happen at about the four-month mark.

$A$s a rule, babies learn from mistakes faster than their parents do.

When you go to another person's home during this phase of your child's life, bring along something she is familiar with—an activity gym, for example. This way, if she gets cranky, you can put her in a familiar, soothing surrounding until she calms down.

If you are trying to give your baby medicine, use a nipple! Babies will suck the medicine from a nipple as though it were breast milk or formula, without knowing the difference.

**"**If it ain't broke, don't fix it." If baby is sleeping well and acting happy, don't change a single thing!

If an outfit is too big but has feet sewn into it, put it on your baby anyway. Then put a sock over each foot of the outfit.

If the outfit is too small, cut out the feet.

You can't control a lot of what happens around your baby, including noise. One of the most important advantages of leaving on a fan while your baby sleeps is that if the telephone rings, a car alarm goes off or a fire truck goes by, your baby will not wake up.

$O$nce you give your baby juice, you can kiss those easy, sleep-inducing bottles of warm breast milk or formula good-bye. Babies usually prefer juice once they have tried it.

Babies love rattles. Rattles help them build dexterity with their hands. Make sure you give your baby a variety to experiment with.

Limit yourself to doing laundry one day a week—otherwise you will go crazy.

Feed your baby when he is hungry. He is growing! (He has the rest of his life to diet.)

Don't take your child for car rides to get her to sleep. It is a dangerous practice and it develops bad habits. If this is how you get your baby to sleep, you might as well start a taxi service, because now you will have to drive your wonderful baby someplace every time you want her to sleep, anyway.

If company is over and you meet your husband in the baby's room for a private conversation, don't forget . . . the monitor is always on!

Trust your instincts!

# Index

# Look for These Baby Tips™ Books & Other Fine Fisher Books Titles